ESTRENO Collection of Contemporary Spanish Plays

General Editor: Martha T. Halsey

TRAIN TO KIU

ALFONSO VALLEJO

TRAIN TO KIU

(El cero transparente)

Translated by H. Rick Hite

ESTRENO
University Park, Pennsylvania
1996

ESTRENO Contemporary Spanish Plays 9
General Editor: Martha T. Halsey
                   Department of Spanish, Italian and Portuguese
                   College of the Liberal Arts
                   The Pennsylvania State University
                   University Park PA 16802 USA

Cataloging Data
Vallejo, Alfonso, 1943-
      Train to Kiu
      Translation of: El cero transparente
      Contents: Train to Kiu
      1. Vallejo, Alfonso, 1943- Translation, English
I. Hite, H. Rick II. Title.
Library of Congress Catalog Card No.: 95-61854
ISBN: 0-9631212-9-4

Original play © Alfonso Vallejo: El cero transparente, 1977.

Translation © H. Rick Hite 1995

The publishers wish to acknowledge with thanks
financial assistance for this translation from the
Dirección General del Libro y Biblioticas
of the Ministerio de Cultura de España.

Cover: Jeffrey Eads

A NOTE ON THE PLAY

"The power of a scream is immeasurable. It doesn't
require spilling a single drop of blood."

Holmes,
Train to Kiu, Part II

Public transportation can be risky! We are at the mercy of officials who, though nominally there to serve us, can seem more bent on extorting our meek compliance. We sit in intimate quarters with unbidden fellow travelers, forced to bear each other's idiosyncrasies (why have I never noticed "idiot" lurking in that word before?). And what more impregnable authority figure can one conjure than the loudspeaker: aloof, imperturbable, exquisite in its absurd logic!

Alfonso Vallejo has chosen this familiar, even banal, situation for the often startlingly original context of his play. The destination is "Kiu," a place re-imagined upon the arrival of each new passenger--four in all (though one is really an angel, or about to become one). Act one, at the station as the compartment fills, is mostly driven by dark laughter. (Holmes to Foster: "I was asking myself why there's no mirror where you live.")

The train lurches off, and we are into the second act. It is here, shortly after the arrival of the mysterious Carol, that Vallejo achieves one of the most breathtakingly fluid transpositions of tone that I have encountered in a play. This carload of fools whose hell-is-others slapstick dance had us laughing before, becomes unified by a growing sense of the need for compassion as the imposed reality of what Kiu represents becomes more clear. Choosing to *share* their suffering rather than *inflict* it, they reach a moment of human dignity before the cruel absurdities of their lot force them (seemingly, perhaps) apart.

Ever mindful of Vallejo's cultural antecedents (Goya, García Lorca, Buñuel, the Picasso of *Guernica*), this pungently lyrical translation by Rick Hite also captures the originality of Vallejo's vision with dialogue that aches to be on the lips of good actors. Perhaps this publication will lead to that.

Rick Seyford
Department of Theater
Mary Baldwin College

ALFONSO VALLEJO

ABOUT THE PLAYWRIGHT

Alfonso Rodríguez Vallejo, better known as Alfonso Vallejo, is a poet, painter, and playwright. He was born in Santander in 1943. He studied in Madrid at the Instituto Francés and at the Universidad Complutense where he received his M.D. in 1966. He is currently Professor of Pathological Medicine at the Universidad Complutense.

He wrote his first play, *Cycle*, in French, in 1961, while a student, and directed a production at the Instituto Francés. Since then he has written over thirty scripts, two-thirds of which have received productions, numbers of which have been outside of Spain, including such far-flung venues as London, New York, Caracas, Milan, and Plock, Poland (see ESTRENO, Spring 1992). Most notable among his plays are *El desguace* (1974; *Breakup*) which received the Lope de Vega Prize in 1977, *Acido sulfúrico* (1975; *Sulphuric Acid*) a runner up for the same prize in 1976, *A tumba abierta* (1976; *By the Open Grave*) which received the Tirso de Molina Prize in 1978, and the play here translated, *El cero transparente* (1977; *Train to Kiu*) which received the Fastenraht Prize of the Spanish Royal Academy in 1981. Other works (with year when written) which have received productions are *Latidos* (1975; *Heartbeats*), *Monólogo para seis voces sin sonido* (1976; *Monologue for Six Voices without Sound*), *Infratonos* (1978; *Infratones*), *La espalda del círculo* (1978; *The Back of the Circle*), *Cangrejos de pared* (1979; *Wall Crabs*), *Orquideas y panteras* (1982; *Orchids and Panthers*), *Gaviotas subterráneas* (1983; *Underground Gulls*), *Monkeys* (1984), *Week-End* (1985), *Espacio interior* (1986; *Interior Space*), and *Fly-by* (1986). Many of his plays have been published in Madrid, principally by Editorial Fundamentos and in collections such as La Avispa, Biblioteca Antonio Machado de Teatro, Arte Escénica, and in *Primer Acto*.

In addition to his playwriting, Alfonso Vallejo has published six volumes of poetry and has had several individual exhibitions of his paintings in both Zaragoza and Madrid.

Inquiries regarding permissions should be addressed to the author through the
Sociedad General de Autores de España
Fernando VI, 4
28004 Madrid, Spain

or to the author through the translator:
Department of Theater
Virginia Wesleyan College
Norfolk, VA 23502

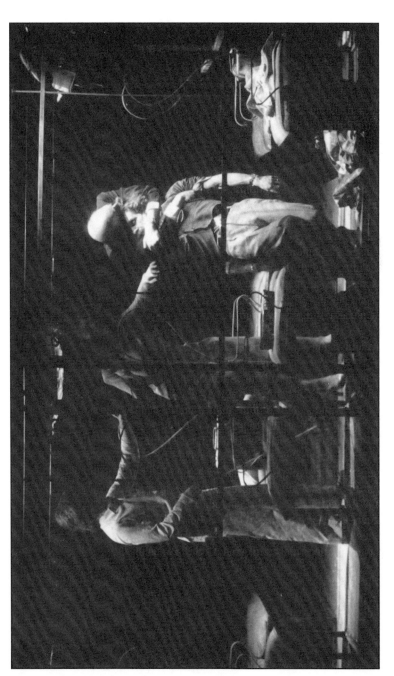

El cero transparente. Teatro del Círculo de Bellas Artes, Madrid, 1980, directed by William Layton.

CHARACTERS

BABINSKI
HOLMES
FOSTER
SIMON
CAROL
DOCTOR
DOCTOR'S ASSISTANT
VOICE OVER LOUDSPEAKER

PART ONE

Empty stage excepting two long seats facing each other and slightly raked toward the audience. We find ourselves in a European train compartment. Screaming train whistles and the sounds of a train station loudspeaker. The audience is placed just off one of the platforms. At the foot of the door to the compartment, in uniform, with a passenger list, a corpulent type with a stony appearance, unshaven, dirty. BABINSKI. Holmes appears from the side. On his right is someone accompanying him who never speaks. They approach BABINSKI.

HOLMES (*Radiantly happy*): A perfect day! Isn't it? (*Silence. BABINSKI stares at him.*) Didn't you hear me? Don't you think it's a perfect day? Huh? (*BABINSKI stares at him and starts humming.*) Are you deaf? Didn't you hear me? (*BABINSKI takes the ticket which HOLMES is carrying and looks at it carefully.*) Do you understand what I'm saying? Is this the train to Kiu? (*BABINSKI looks at him, smiles without saying a word.*) I'm asking you if this is the train for Kiu? Answer me!

BABINSKI (*To the man accompanying HOLMES*): You can go now. (*The man leaves.*) (*Screaming.*) Yes! This is it, stupid! And the weather is not perfect in my opinion. (*Unbuttoning his collar.*) It's a lousy day.

HOLMES: Listen...

BABINSKI: Why should I listen?

HOLMES: You're not going to put me in a bad mood. Not a bit! For me today is a specially happy day.

BABINSKI: Not for me.

HOLMES: Fine. I see there's no talking with you. When do we get to Kiu?

BABINSKI: Depends.

HOLMES: On what?

BABINSKI: On when we get there.

HOLMES: If you're trying to make fun of me.

BABINSKI: Besides, we don't always get there.

HOLMES: What do you mean?

BABINSKI: Kiu's a long way. A very long way! And the trip is hard. Very hard trip! You have to cross ranges of mountains, mesetas, crags, knolls, buttes, and stonescapes. Hills and hillocks, massifs, fords, terrible precipices...

HOLMES: Please...

BABINSKI: Entire orographical systems, with all their derivations! And not perpendicularly, but longitudinally, you know what I mean? From the first to the last mountain. The layout for the line to Kiu wasn't done scientifically as you might suppose, friend. No, nothing of the sort. The layout for the line to Kiu was one piss poor job. A fuck up. Did you know that?

HOLMES (*Perplexed*): No. I...

BABINSKI: Well, now you know it! You've gone a little pale, huh? (*Smiling sadistically.*) You weren't expecting that, right?

HOLMES (*With menace*): If you're trying to make a fool of me. If for some reason I don't know about, you think for a moment you can...

BABINSKI (*Interrupting him*): I know very well what gloomy thoughts are seething around in that confused head. (*He grabs the index finger HOLMES is shaking at him threateningly, and sticks it in his mouth.*)

HOLMES (*Pulling his finger out*): You don't know anything! You! You put one of my fingers in your mouth again, and I'll kill you!

BABINSKI: You're thinking... but aren't there tunnels? And I answer: of course, there are tunnels! Many, many, many! Droves of tunnels. But they're not always passable. Ah, no! Sometimes terrible landslides tear the rails to pieces. Yes, friend! You have to travel to Kiu with the utmost care, holding your breath, like on a high wire. At the slightest false move... Crash! Whole mountains tumble down on the train.

HOLMES: You're crazy.

BABINSKI: Crazy, right? And those horrible, hair-raising masses of ice, huh?

HOLMES: What are you talking about?

BABINSKI: Those gigantean frosts that cover over the stations along the way, huh? The train crawls along, whistling. Whee! whee! That puny, scarey whistle, full of anguish. Nothing! You look around. Nothing! As if the snow has swallowed up everything. Nothing. Not a living soul, not a breath of life. No smoke, no anything. Nothing but nothing! Just so you get the picture, imbecile! Just so you know what you're getting into! (*Silence.*) Nothing to say? Right? Are we dumbstruck?

HOLMES: No. They didn't tell me any of that. Just the opposite.

BABINSKI: And that's just the beginning. Because after the ice comes the desert. You didn't know about that either, right?

HOLMES: The desert? What are you talking about?

BABINSKI: What am I talking about? Stupid! You've never seen a desert like it, so empty, so many miles, such an intensity of desert! You enjoy good, strong emotional excitement?

HOLMES (*Grabs BABINSKI by the lapels*): Certainly I enjoy it.

(*He stares with jaws clenched at BABINSKI. HOLMES is a heavy set man with a big moustache. Clear, direct, and aggressive gestures. He is wearing a blue wool suit, very wrinkled. He suggests an enormous capacity for attack.*)

BABINSKI: Well you're going to enjoy some. The place is an oven. A lot of them die from dehydration.

(BABINSKI knocks his hands away with a rap on the wrist. Silence.)

HOLMES: I don't understand. I don't understand. They told me it was a pleasant trip, in a train, the latest model, with air conditioning, a restaurant, attendants.

BABINSKI *(A biting challenge)*: I'm the attendant. *(Silence.)* Only right now I'm disguised as the station boy. *(He hands him a fan with floral design.)* And this is your air conditioning.

HOLMES: They told me...

BABINSKI *(With unusual violence)*: Lies! I know very well what they told you, you stupid fool!

HOLMES: Don't you insult me again!

BABINSKI: What they tell everybody! A rugged, dry landscape, right? Lies! Tunnels and tunnels! *(Covering his ears, imitating the sound of a train.)* Clickety clickety click, clickety clickety click! *(With a grin expressing pain.)* Wheeeee! Wheeeee! *(On the verge of nervous collapse.)* Towns, cities without any sign of life. Death, silence, tunnels, tunnels, endless night scattered with ghosts. You hear me? You hear me? And we're the ghosts! Passengers arguing about the delay, the water, the food. Thirsty, hungry, sexually frustrated, tearing themselves to pieces. On the verge of madness, trying to smash the rigid discipline I have to impose to get us to Kiu. *(Pause.)* And, by the way, I just want to warn you: I am in charge of the train. Is that clear? On route I am the final authority, the supreme and final hierarchical element of this train. You hear me?

HOLMES: I hear you.

BABINSKI: My superiors consider me the ideal man to deal with you people. That's why for ten years I've made this same run. *(He chews on his cigar.)* In the most absolute of solitudes, century after century, morning, noon, and night, month after month, year after year. With my head full of noises, without family, without friends.

HOLMES: Fine. You're starting to make me tired, fellow. I didn't come here to listen to you complain. *(He climbs into the train.)* I came here to get some rest.

BABINSKI: Really?

HOLMES: I need to get some rest! Urgently! I... I'm on vacation.

BABINSKI: We'll keep that in mind, friend. We'll see what kind of rest is in store for you.

HOLMES: What do you mean?

BABINSKI: Nothing. You're the window seat on the left.

HOLMES (*Defiantly*): We certainly will see.

BABINSKI: Yea, we'll see. We certainly will. This is only just getting started.

(*HOLMES enters the compartment, sits down, looks around worriedly. FOSTER enters from side, accompanied by a silent figure.*)

FOSTER (*To the person accompanying him*): Thank you very much, sir. I am enormously grateful to you for accompanying me. Without you I'd never have found the station. (*Offers his hand.*) Thank you again. (*The man accompanying FOSTER exits.*) (*To BABINSKI.*) Pardon me, sir. Is this the train for Kiu?

BABINSKI (*Chewing furiously on his cigar*): Kee.

FOSTER: Kiu?

BABINSKI (*Looking him up and down*): Kaa.

FOSTER: I don't understand you, I'm sorry. Are you Japanese?

BABINSKI: Kiu.

FOSTER: Exactly. Yes, the train to Kiu. That's what I'm asking you. (*With emphasis.*) Kiu?

BABINSKI: Koh.

FOSTER: This is maddening! Kaa. Koh. Kee! What language is this? (*BABINSKI shows his teeth.*) But... Now, that's enough!

BABINSKI: Right! Not normal! Kee! Kaa! Koh! Kee! Get it? Get out of here with your idiot load of talk! (*Grabbing him by the arm.*) Get in!

FOSTER: Just a moment!

BABINSKI: Moment nothing! Get in! (*Gives him a shove.*)

FOSTER (*Livid*): Don't you touch me again. Animal!. I've asked you for information, and it's your obligation to give it to me. I'm a sick man. I... I'm diabetic.

BABINSKI: And me?

FOSTER: And I have high blood pressure. And gout. And cirrhosis. And encephalitis.

BABINSKI: And me? Me, I'm dying too. Nobody's got it over me with sickness.

FOSTER (*Louder, irritated*): My hearing is poor, I scarcely eat, my father was a plumber, and my mother a whore! My grandfather ran a circus.

BABINSKI (*Sweating*): Can it! (*He grabs him suddenly and shoves him into the train.*) And mine ran a flop-house! (*Shuts the door.*)

FOSTER (*From the corridor, gesticulating*): Jackass! Clodhopper! Prissy boy! I intend to report you! You have to tell me this! It's your obligation!

BABINSKI: What do you want to know?

FOSTER: If this is the train for Kiu?

BABINSKI: Kiu.

FOSTER (*Beating on the window*): Never mind Kiu! Just yes or no! Just a normal, sensible person's answer! Kiu, Kaa, Kee, Koh! Either yes or no!

BABINSKI: So, yes! Yes! You deaf post! Detritus! Bag of crap! Poor fellow! Anything else?

FOSTER: He's unhinging me! This guy! Is there... is there a restaurant?

BABINSKI: I'm the restaurant.

FOSTER: Imbecile! Give me a straight answer! I need to know what I've gotten into. I want to know everything: arrival time, departure time, weather report. If there's air conditioning!

BABINSKI: I'm the air conditioning.

FOSTER (*Trying without effect to open the corridor window*): I'll kill you, you shitboy! You won't come out of this trip alive! You garbage! Bonehead pervert, shit-eating, tit-sucking, son of a bitch! (*Beating on the window.*) Damn window! I'll break it! Get me out of here!

BABINSKI: Easy. Take it easy now. The windows don't work.

FOSTER (*Pressing his ear against it.*): What?

BABINSKI: Take a deep breath while you can. Cool down. You'll see soon enough when we get to the desert. Out there the mosquitoes are big as pigeons.

FOSTER: What did you say about pigeons? Speak louder!

BABINSKI: Never mind pigeons! In the desert the mosquitoes are as big as... as rabbits! No, bigger, even bigger! Big as sheep! With one bite they can finish off a man.

(*BABINSKI walks along the platform, his hands behind his back. FOSTER nervously follows down the train corridor, trying to catch what he is saying.*)

BABINSKI: And as for the waters there, at Kiu. (*Laughs.*)

FOSTER: And what's wrong with the waters? Huh?

BABINSKI: They're not really good for the gout.

FOSTER: They're not? And what are they good for?

BABINSKI: They cause gout.

FOSTER (*Hitting the window*): You pig!

BABINSKI: And they'll be curtains for your high blood pressure and diabetes. (*Making a thumbs down gesture.*) You'll never make it, friend.

(*FOSTER gives him the finger.*)

FOSTER: We'll see, you dumb fuck.

BABINSKI: What did you call me? Young buck?

FOSTER (*With exaggerated mouthing but in a stage whisper*): You're not going to poison my vacation, you clod son of a whore-bitch.

BABINSKI: Vocalize! Speak up! So I can make you out!

FOSTER (*Lowering his voice even more*): You made me out all right. Your father was a prissy pimp and your mother, a bongo drummer in a colored band. (*Obscene arm-cutting gesture.*)

BABINSKI: If I come in there. By God, I swear!

FOSTER: Kee? I can't hear you. (*Putting his hands to his ears and moving them like wings, laughing.*)

BABINSKI: By God, you'll remember me!

(*FOSTER sticks his index fingers in his ears and sticks out his tongue.*)

FOSTER: I've just broken off all relations with you, my fine fellow. Please, contact me only by mail.

(*FOSTER enters the compartment where he finds HOLMES. He sits down. Silence.*)

FOSTER: Are you going to Kiu?

HOLMES: Kee.

FOSTER: Another one. O.K!

HOLMES: Kaa!

FOSTER: Kaa, kaa, cock-a-doodle-doo! Shit on you! They're making me turn into some bad mannered boor. Me, who's always been so proper about my manners.

HOLMES: Cock.

FOSTER: Cunt!

HOLMES: Pity we don't understand each other! With the trip that's ahead of us. Did you hear about the mosquitoes?

FOSTER: You don't speak my language?

HOLMES: No. (*Pause.*) Do you, mine?

FOSTER: Neither.

HOLMES: You see? I don't know how we'll understand each other.

FOSTER: It's all the same if we don't understand each other.

HOLMES: I see your point. So much the better, because your face looks like...

FOSTER: Like what? What's wrong with my face?

HOLMES: Do you mind if I tell you?

FOSTER: Go on.

HOLMES: I hope you won't think me impertinent.

FOSTER: Not at all! Say it!

HOLMES: Aren't there any mirrors where you live?

FOSTER: Why do you ask that?

HOLMES: I don't say this to be critical. But you have a booger sticking under your left eye. (*FOSTER, after observing HOLMES carefully, gets up, looks in the mirror, and wipes his face with a handkerchief.*)

FOSTER: Funny place for a booger, isn't it? You'd think my boogers had legs. (*Smiles.*)

HOLMES: Do they?

FOSTER (*Looking at it*): No. (*He stands there not knowing what to do with the booger in his hand. Then he turns around and throws it over his shoulder.*) Hup! (*He sits down again. Silence. HOLMES keeps looking at him.*) Now what?

HOLMES: There's more.

FOSTER: What? More?

HOLMES: You've got another one under your right ear.

(*FOSTER jumps up and looks at himself again.*)

FOSTER: So there is! Got it! I can't figure how he could've gotten to such an unlikely place. But no doubt about it now: my boogers are itinerant boogers. That's quite clear. (*He throws it on the floor and steps on it hard. He sits down again. Silence. HOLMES continues looking at him.*) Do you want to tell me once and for all: what the matter is with you? Why are you looking at me so much? Maybe you fancy me? Maybe you like little boys or something?

HOLMES: I can't find the words. Really, this is not meant in the sense of criticism, but I think I have an obligation to tell you. (*Pause.*) Why do you wear such awful colored underpants? (*FOSTER looks down at his open fly.*)

FOSTER: Hello! (*Zips up.*) Forgive me, please. I didn't do that with any provocative intentions, I assure you.

HOLMES: In any case it wouldn't have provoked me.

FOSTER: It's just that... Well... I'm not an obsessive about personal tidiness. (*HOLMES keeps looking at him.*) You don't believe me? Why are you looking at me now?

HOLMES (*Very serious*): I was asking myself why there's no mirror where you live.

FOSTER (*Serious*): Ask yourself that.

HOLMES: You're not a vagrant.

FOSTER: No.

HOLMES: Your suit, nice fabric. Acceptable cut. Your hands are delicate. Perhaps belonging to a studious type? (*Pause.*) Where are you from?

FOSTER: I'm from where I'm from, and I'm going to where I'm going. Like you. Like everyone.

HOLMES: Why does it bother you that I ask where you're from?

FOSTER: I'm sorry. I don't understand what you're saying. We're not the same nationality. I'm sorry. (*He looks out the window. Silence.*)

HOLMES: Are you going to Kiu?

FOSTER: Yes.

(*Silence. FOSTER is a cachectic type, tall, emaciated, with glasses. He's long limbed, and his movements are guarded. His green eyes have an intelligent, somewhat childlike look. His movements and attitudes suggest something delicately human, simpatico, and hot blooded. His outbursts of high spirits alternate with periods of staring into space with a vague, sad, painful grin on his face.*)

FOSTER: You won't believe this, but today is the first day in a good many years which really belongs to me. I've been under some unusual and heavy pressure which just about did me in . The little of me I had left. (*Pause.*) Today is my first day of genuine happiness. Fact is I've left behind some terrible stuff. Some dark, borderline situations that could well have done me in. (*Pause.*) Today I feel like the world is starting all over for me. Like it's starting to move ahead again, on this train, towards Kiu. That tremendous, astonishing city where I'm hoping to reconcile myself with life, finally, and maybe, for the first time. (*Pause.*) All I want is to get there and to take off my clothes and to walk out into the water. Ever since I was a child, I've had a fierce devotion to the sea. (*Pause.*) Besides, swimming is my favorite sport.

HOLMES: Are you sure you'll be able to swim? My information has it that Kiu is in the mountains.

FOSTER: You're a little strange.

HOLMES: Don't you believe it!

FOSTER: I believe maybe you're a little crazy. Saying Kiu is in the mountains. (*Pause.*) And your way of looking at me. Your questions.

HOLMES: They've shown me photographs.

FOSTER: Me too. Beautiful photographs of the beaches, with the emerald sea and the crashing waves, encircled by giant palms and lush, astonishing greenery. In Kiu...

HOLMES (*Interrupting him*): I've seen photographs of the mountains. (*Pause.*) Are you sure we're talking about the same city?

FOSTER: I think so. But. There can't be mountains. They've assured me.

HOLMES: They've assured me that in Kiu there were deep, lush valleys, covered with astonishing greenery. That the waters at Kiu have an extraordinary clarity. That they rise from high rock springs and are crystalline pure. That in Kiu there are all varieties of fruit, the air is warm, the climate, sweetly temperate. They've told me. They've assured me that everything in Kiu would seem to be built to human scale, that nature there seems to well up with rare strength resembling that of Paradise. That's what Kiu is like. Exactly that. They've assured me that there life is possible. And not a life intended for nothing. Like the life we're living now.

(*HOLMES wipes the sweat from his brow and neck with a handkerchief. His tone has changed to one of profound anguish and emotion.*)

HOLMES: And the fact is, my friend, that I have an urgent need for all this. I have also been under some unusual pressure. I... I have this urgent need to get myself free. And. (*Pause. Again wiping away sweat. He sits for a few moments entirely quiet, looking intensely at FOSTER.*)

FOSTER: Bucolic description.

HOLMES: You think so?

FOSTER: It seems. It almost seems as if you've been making it all up, the city, over some period of time. Making it all up to fit yourself.

HOLMES (*Serious*): Who are you?

FOSTER: Now they've told me that the men in Kiu, after they eat, take a nap, just indolently sitting around on the ground.

HOLMES: No!

FOSTER: Yes!

HOLMES (*In a doubtful tone*): That would be hard on the old behind. wouldn't it? (*Smiling.*) Why don't they get into bed?

FOSTER: You always fix on the least important thing. Like boogers on my face, like my fly is open, like their butts might hurt! So how should I know if they hurt! Don't ask me! Ask them! When you get there. Don't you understand that not going to bed is no indication that they don't have any place to sleep?

HOLMES: No?

FOSTER: It's. It's because. Because in Kiu they're living. The way nature intended. Idiot! And besides, every once in a while... (*Gesturing.*) They brush away flies with their hand, one by one, because they're in no hurry, because for centuries they've been cultivating the highest form of art: the art of living! In Kiu...

HOLMES: Ah! O.K., I understand. It's all the same to me if they don't have behinds.

FOSTER: Will you let me tell you once and for all what they told me?

HOLMES: Kee.

FOSTER: Cut that crap! Kee. Speak English!

HOLMES: What did they tell you?

FOSTER (*Absolutely screaming*): They told me that the people in Kiu all love each other deeply, and that the sun is always shining, and that the inhabitants, although living in absolute poverty. Are all what? Do you know?

HOLMES: Hungry?

FOSTER: What's gotten into you all of a sudden? (*Pause.*) They are all filled with faith, a blind faith in the light. Blockhead! A confidence in the light! Like a sublime sixth sense for the light! The light for them is like some gift of nature that life has given them. Some superior faculty of reconciliation with humanity!

HOLMES: You're making me deaf! (*Yelling.*) Stop yelling at me!

FOSTER: I'll yell as much as I want! I am free! You understand me? I'm free! And I have come out into the world to yell about it! (*Yells.*) And you're making me lose my patience, you. Troglodyte! (*He gets up furiously.*)

HOLMES: Your fly's open again.

FOSTER: I don't give a damn! (*He gives the zipper a good yank, and lets out a scream of pain.*) That was your fault. (*Grimacing with pain, his hand on his genitals, he goes into the corridor.*)

HOLMES: You're leaving?

FOSTER: Yes! Just the sight of you and I'm quite capable of killing myself. You lumpish brute!

(*He fumes off down the corridor. The noise of doors is heard. Moments later he comes back, enters the compartment, and sits down, impassive.*)

FOSTER: All the compartments are locked. But had I found any little corner to crouch in. I would have crouched in it. I swear. (*Silence.*)

HOLMES: Will it bother you if I tell you there's another booger sticking on your face?

FOSTER (*Leaps up, tearing at his hair*): Nooooo! But let's see! Where are so many boogers coming from? And look at the boogers! Just look at them! (*Looking in the mirror.*) And my fly's open again! (*Pulling little things off his face.*) And another one! And another! Yes indeedy! I am just one heap of rotting boogers! Well then. Whatever. Just don't direct another word to me, for the rest of your life! I hate you!

HOLMES: Are you the police?

FOSTER: Me? (*Sits down on the other side of the compartment.*) No! And I do not wish to speak with you ever again. Is that clear?

HOLMES: Agreed.

(*FOSTER, nervous, takes out a cigarette and, trembling, puts it in his mouth. He searches for matches without success. Silence. He mops the sweat.*)

FOSTER: Listen. (*Silence.*) Listen. Please, could you give me a light?

HOLMES: Kee?

FOSTER: I need a cigarette! My nerves are about to explode! (*He reaches for the cigar which HOLMES has just lighted.*)

HOLMES: No! No light! You have to ask me for a light. On your knees. Otherwise.

FOSTER: That your eyes will never see. Cretin! Before that. Death.

(*Silence. He searches desperately for a match. Then, submissively, he gets down on his knees without saying a word, and HOLMES lights his cigarette.*)

HOLMES: Tobacco will be the ruin of you. (*FOSTER takes greedy drags, coughing heavily.*)

FOSTER: Do you know why I'm going to Kiu?

HOLMES: No.

FOSTER: To die. (*Pause.*) I am already disintegrating.

HOLMES: Come on.

FOSTER: It's hard to admit, but I am. (*Pause.*) I went into the bathroom with the intention of shaving. And I looked at myself in the mirror. And I noticed something amazing: my face is coming loose. I wanted to scream, and I couldn't. I tried to touch my eyes, and I couldn't find them. I spoke to the things around me, but they didn't recognize me. My body had turned sick from suffering. I needed air. I could not have lived one day more without freedom.

(*Silence. FOSTER'S face is pale, distorted, his breathing hard.*)

HOLMES: Where were you?

FOSTER: Then one of my kidneys came loose and made a sound inside my abdomen like dry leaves. My body was breaking to pieces, crumbling to dust. It was dying on me. (*Pause.*) Why did you ask me before if I were the police? (*Pause.*) Were you afraid of something?

(*Silence.*)

HOLMES: Are you sure that Kiu exists?

FOSTER: Yes. I think it does.

HOLMES: You're sure you weren't making it up?

FOSTER: They've only ever talked to me about it through insinuations. I don't have a very concrete idea about where I'm going. But then I've always gone about inventing the cities I've passed through. I've been living in an unreal world for a long time. I mean. In my delusions. Inventing myself. (*Pause.*) I've been in a mental hospital. Today is my first day of release.

(*Silence. HOLMES and FOSTER sit silently absorbed, motionless, their expressions serious and worried.*)

LOUDSPEAKER (*A woman's voice*): Attention passengers. The train to Kiu is ready for departure. The management of this line would like to wish you luck. We have no intentions of deceiving you: you are about to undertake more of an adventure than a trip. The company, while reminding you that it accepts no responsibility for the morale and physical welfare of the passengers, asks that you pardon the inconveniences you are about to experience, namely, the lack of even the barest of necessities, the absence of restaurant, air conditioning, and lavatories; the brutishness of the employees and the wretched condition of the train. At the same time we should like to stop certain absurd rumors which have lately been propagated. The train to Kiu is not a death-train. The train to Kiu arrives in Kiu, sooner or later, as the case may be. But it always arrives. On that point, ladies and gentlemen, we would not deceive you. We remain mindful of our responsibility.

(*Silence. HOLMES and FOSTER look at each other. They get up.*)

FOSTER: But.

(*BABINSKI enters.*)

BABINSKI: Can't you read what's posted? (*Points to an old notice, taking FOSTER'S cigarette from his mouth, throwing it on the floor, and stepping on it.*) No Smoking. No Smoking! It says that very clearly, I believe.

FOSTER: But... This is unheard of!

BABINSKI (*Moving toward HOLMES*): Give me that cigar.

HOLMES: No.

BABINSKI: I'm telling you: give me that cigar!

HOLMES: No! No! I won't give it to you! Never!

(*He takes it out of his mouth and tries to hide it. BABINSKI wrestles with him.*)

HOLMES: Stop it! Are you crazy? I won't give it to you!

(*Just when BABINSKI is at the point of getting it, HOLMES tosses it to FOSTER. Then FOSTER to HOLMES and HOLMES back to FOSTER. The cigar disappears. BABINSKI gives them both a hard look.*)

BABINSKI: The cigar.

HOLMES: What cigar?

FOSTER: I don't have anything. I don't know anything.

BABINSKI: That cigar better show up right now!

HOLMES: Go look for it!

(*BABINSKI bites his lower lip, turns, and goes towards the door. From behind him FOSTER sticks his tongue out at him and gestures with his hands. BABINSKI suddenly swings around and grabs FOSTER by the lapels.*)

BABINSKI: What did you do? Cretin!

FOSTER: Me? Nothing!

BABINSKI: I saw you in the window! You stuck your tongue out at me!

FOSTER: Me? That's a lie!

BABINSKI: The truth!

FOSTER: I swear, on my mother's grave!

BABINSKI: Swear be damned! You stuck your tongue out at me!

FOSTER: I swear, on my father's grave!

HOLMES: Listen! I don't believe this!

(*At that moment SIMON appears at the door. A tall, thin, elegant individual with black hair combed straight back, dark glasses and a white cane. It is immediately apparent that he is blind. He enters the compartment colliding forcefully against BABINSKI who lets out a scream of pain.*)

SIMON: I beg your pardon. I'm sincerely sorry.

BABINSKI: You stepped on my foot! You did that on purpose!

SIMON: No, sir. I'm blind. I repeat: I'm sorry.

BABINSKI: Who are you?

SIMON: What?

BABINSKI: Your name! (*Looking at his list.*) Come on! Quick!

SIMON: I'm sorry. I'm also deaf. I can't hear a thing. You'll have to forgive me. I'm a wreck. I can hear you're shouting, but I don't understand what you're saying. Forgive me, gentlemen.

BABINSKI (*Cupping his hands and yelling into his ear*): Stupid booby! Your naaaaaame!

SIMON: Come again. What's that? (*Changing position to hear better and stepping on BABINSKI'S other foot. A new scream of pain as BABINSKI hops around the compartment holding his foot.*) Nothing. It's impossible. Not a word. (*He turns suddenly catching BABINSKI in the face with his cane. A fresh outcry of pain and rage.*) Did that catch somebody? I'm sorry. I assure you, I am sorry, gentlemen. Now I'll just get myself seated. And I won't move anymore. (*Sitting down and putting his hands on his cane, completely unperturbed.*)

BABINSKI (*Furiously grabbing SIMON by the jacket and raising his fist*): You!

HOLMES (*Grabbing BABINSKI's wrist with real force*): Don't you think that's enough? He's blind.

BABINSKI: Let go of me!

(*HOLMES grabs his other wrist with incredible force. BABINSKI cannot pull himself free.*)

HOLMES: Would you like to quiet down? He didn't try to step on your foot.

FOSTER: When we get to Kiu, I intend to report him to the authorities. They should know about this! Pushy brute. Prepuce!

BABINSKI: What did you say about precious? What did you call me?

FOSTER: Look. I...

BABINSKI: Well, you know what I say to you? You know my answer to you! Give me that hand. (*Grabbing his hand, he pulls it to his rear-end and lets go with a terrific peacemaker blast.*)

FOSTER: Oh!

BABINSKI (*He sticks his tongue out at him. Then to HOLMES.*): And as for you, my pretty gentleman. You better be ready. This is a very long trip, and my recourse to meanness is tremendous. Look. (*Pulling up his shirt.*) Scars! All over! From a lot of fights! From knives, from pistols! Look, stupid. Scars and more scars. (*Pulling down his pants.*) And here, another one. (*Turning around.*) Get a good look at them, cretin. (*Letting off another blast.*) You don't know who you've come up against. (*He starts out, haughtily.*)

LOUDSPEAKER: Mr Babinski! Mr Babinski! Report at once to Control! On the double!

BABINSKI: Again! You're trying to kill me.

LOUDSPEAKER (*Always a woman's voice*): Mr Babinski, report to Control!

BABINSKI (*Screaming at the loudspeaker*): I'm coming already!

LOUDSPEAKER: Ill-bred!

BABINSKI: Filthy sow!

LOUDSPEAKER: Sow? Get up here at once, or no departure.

BABINSKI: Oh no?. You filthy. I'll drag your... Vicious!

(*BABINSKI exits running in the direction of Control. Silence.*)

SIMON (*Stretching his neck out like a dog sniffing*): Is there anyone else here with you two?

HOLMES: No.

FOSTER: But.

SIMON: Strange. Is there much time before we leave?

FOSTER: He can hear!

HOLMES: He hears perfectly. Are you at least blind?

SIMON: Yes. Unfortunately.

FOSTER: Were you waiting for someone?

SIMON: Well. Yes. I think so. You haven't seen anyone come through? A young woman. Very beautiful. Someone...

FOSTER: No.

HOLMES: No one has come through. And we've been here a good while.

SIMON: It's all right.

(*FOSTER and HOLMES look at each other not knowing quite how to react to SIMON'S presence which has something strange about it: motionless, delicate, inner, as if hanging on the slightest noise or movement.*)

HOLMES: Are you going to Kiu?

SIMON: Yes.
FOSTER: Do you know Kiu?
SIMON: No. (*Pause.*) Are there any more people in this coach?
HOLMES: I don't think so. The other compartments are locked.

(*Silence.*)

SIMON: She... She's a tall woman. Blonde. Slender. Exceptionally beautiful.
Are you certain you haven't seen her?
HOLMES: Yes.
SIMON: Forgive me for going on, but it's very important to me. I've been... I've
been looking for this person for a long time. And I know that she has to be
on this train today. You didn't happen to see her on the platform? Or getting
into another coach? Perhaps...
FOSTER: Sorry. No.
HOLMES: Me neither. I'm sure. But... can I ask you something? I'm sort of
curious. How can you be looking for her if you're blind?

(*Silence.*)

SIMON: It's a reasonable question. Really. (*Pause.*) And. I don't know
whether you're going to believe this, but I look for her by listening to birds.
Singing. (*Pause.*) You see. Of course you couldn't know this, but I'm
familiar with... I understand the songs of birds. Birds are very effective and
unusual allies.

(*Silence. HOLMES and FOSTER exchange a look.*)

SIMON: The language of birds is an intelligent and prophetic language, full of
meaning, but difficult to understand.

(*Silence.*)

FOSTER: Would you perhaps have a picture of her? Something. It's possible
that I've seen her and didn't realize it. Maybe I could remember her.

(*SIMON takes out a magazine and opens it to the centerfold.*)

SIMON: Do you see her?
FOSTER: Yes.

SIMON: Take it. Look at it closely. (*Silence.*) Do you see her?

HOLMES (*Nonplussed*): Yes. No. I don't think...

SIMON (*Interrupting him in a strangely forceful way*): Naked. Lying there, posed on that red terracotta tile floor. Right?

HOLMES: She is beautiful.

SIMON: Beautiful? Don't you think she's exceptionally beautiful?

FOSTER: Very beautiful, yes, of course.

SIMON: Look at her breasts, her thighs, her mouth, her eyes. Everything. Look. Isn't she an angel? Isn't she absolutely beautiful? Isn't she almost impossible?

FOSTER: Quite noble looking. (*He looks at HOLMES and shrugs his shoulders.*)

SIMON: Angelic expression!

FOSTER: Just what I meant.

SIMON: She's my guardian angel. Not a creature of flesh and blood, no. She seems real, but that's only appearance. (*Pause.*) I know who she really is. I'm the only one who knows her true nature.

(*Silence. HOLMES, intrigued, crosses his legs without taking his eyes off SIMON. Suddenly the door opens and CAROL ROSENBAUM comes in. She is an exceptionally beautiful woman, blonde, exuberant, strong, refined, angelic.*)

SIMON (*Stretching his neck forward, nosing the air. Silence.*): Who came in? (*Silence.*) Who?

CAROL: May I sit down?

(*Silence. She's wearing sunglasses. HOLMES and FOSTER observe her.*)

CAROL: Is something wrong, gentlemen? Why are you looking at me like that?

FOSTER (*Shaking his head as if to clear it*): I beg your pardon, Miss. Just a simple confusion. We were just talking about... about... But, it doesn't matter. For a moment there...

HOLMES: Please, sit down. Please, allow me.

(*He situates CAROL'S suitcase, then sits down and begins to read. For the first time the noise of birds is heard. Then silence again. CAROL has sat down opposite SIMON.*)

SIMON: Hello.

CAROL (*Surprised*): Hello. (*Silence.*)

SIMON: I didn't think you would get here. The train's about to leave.
CAROL: I don't understand. Have we seen each other before?
SIMON: You don't know me. (*Silence.*)
CAROL: And you know me?
SIMON: Yes.
CAROL: Well then.

(*Silence. Suddenly the whole set lurches. Strange machine noises, part animal, part steel, as the train sets itself in motion. Jerks, sparks, flickering of lights. BABINSKI, disheveled, enters the corridor, buttoning up his fly.*)

CAROL: Well then?

(*BABINSKI opens the door and looks in with a horsey smile. A shrill whistle. Sparks flying.*)

PART TWO

Powerful sound of the train roaring through tunnel after tunnel, its whistle screaming, towards some destination unknown even to it; whistling through dead cities, almost unreal, covered over by gigantic ice formations. Mixed with this is the sound of the wind gusting, bone chilling, deadly, whispering, and whining. The light entering through the windows is a cold, nocturnal light, crepuscular, dying. Everyone is sitting motionless. When someone speaks, the rest remain motionless, absorbed in thought, as if not hearing. A strange atmosphere of withdrawal, silent and heavy, has taken them over. Every noise counts. Every insinuation of movement counts. SIMON and CAROL are seated opposite each other.

CAROL: Well then?

SIMON: Well then. (*Pause.*) You are an angel come to save me. You speak; but you don't speak. You... what you're saying, you're saying with your hands. You and I will never be separated from each other again. Because I have loved you so deeply. In silence. For so many years.

(The sound of the train is like background music, tenuous and soft, at times disappearing. Pause. CAROL remains motionless, observing SIMON.)

SIMON: You're an apparition, a phantasma. You are a redeeming angel, and you are a fiction. You are my ultimate reality and the culminating point around which my existence circles. Because of you, I exist. And for you, if you would allow, I would die if need be. (*The sound of the train accompanies SIMON, who speaks almost without moving the muscles of his face, imperturbable, serious, like someone setting free words long held in the darkness of thought.*) My devotion to you reaches so far that what seem simple words spoken in haste and by rote are truly cries and inner voices calling for you.

(Silence.)

CAROL: It's so sad that I can't understand you. I don't understand what you're saying. And it would delight me to talk with you. How sad we're so different. How sad we don't speak the same language.

SIMON: Is that true?

CAROL: Don't you think so?

SIMON: It's possible. I don't know.

CAROL: If I could understand you. Even if not everything. Something. A little. It seems so interesting what you're saying. There's so much feeling in your words. It's true, I would like so much to be able to talk with you.

SIMON: What for?

CAROL: I have so much to tell you.

SIMON: For example.

CAROL: That you have a very kind face.

SIMON: Ah.

CAROL: And also that your eyebrows are magnificent. And that your eyes, even though you're wearing dark glasses and you're blind, your eyes must be beautiful. Green, clear, striking.

SIMON: Go on. Go on, please.

CAROL: It's no use, don't you think? We don't speak the same language. I'm sure you don't understand anything I say.

SIMON: It doesn't matter. Go on. I can imagine it.

CAROL (*Smiling*): Well, also... I also want to tell you that you have exceptionally beautiful teeth and that your hands are also beautiful and that it's beautiful also the way your ears are set. (*Pause.*) Anything else?

SIMON: Go on, please, go on.

CAROL: I can't think of anything else.

SIMON (*Full of enthusiasm*): I'm ready to pay you back whatever it takes. I'll sing you a song, whatever you like. But talk to me. I beg you. (*Silence.*) That way... at least... the trip will seem shorter. I mean... (*Silence.*)

CAROL: Why are you talking to me? Why are you saying all of this? Who are you? (*Silence.*)

SIMON: Are you a model?

CAROL: How did you know?

SIMON: Have you ever posed nude?

CAROL: Why do you want to know? Yes, once.

SIMON: I know other things about you. (*Pause.*) You're blonde, you have green eyes, a small nose, your breasts are high and firm, your hips strong, your legs slender, your back straight.

CAROL: A very romantic description.

SIMON: Are you blonde?

CAROL: Yes.

SIMON: Are your green eyes? (*Silence.*) Answer me, please.

CAROL: Yes.

SIMON: Your genitalia are snug, your skin smooth, your neck high. I know exactly what you're like. (*Pause.*) And you're ill, suffering from a sickened sensibility.

CAROL: Please!

SIMON: And from innocence almost unallowable. Your candor is gigantic, your capacity for love, monstrous... you...

CAROL: Listen, please.

SIMON: Don't entreat me. It's no use. My love for you is blind, irrevocable, desperate. Nothing could ever free you from me. (*Pause.*) I want to repeat it a thousand times and more: I love you, Carol.

CAROL: But. How do you know my name?

SIMON: Carol Rosenbaum. (*Pause.*) I've been waiting for you. I knew that today, at last, we would have to meet.

CAROL: Who told you?

SIMON: The birds.

CAROL: Who?

SIMON: The birds. I understand the language of the birds. They're my special allies.

(*Silence. CAROL takes off her glasses and gives SIMON a long look. CAROL cannot be embodied in words, does not express herself in words. Hers is a dramatic presence. The attitudes she strikes, her manner of moving, her splendor and physical sensibility are what form the spine of her character. CAROL feels silence and surprise with her skin. And CAROL is exceptionally thin skinned. The audience should be able to perceive suffering and mystery in her delicate and smooth skin. Her clothes, her manner of dress, her make-up, her extraordinary elegance and bearing, all ought to project her near non-existence.*)

CAROL: You've seen me before?

SIMON: Yes. Well, no. Or maybe, yes. I'm not sure. (*Pause.*) A few years ago you posed nude. You were in a garden, and in the background were giant plants hanging over you. There you were, naked, set there in the midst of that exuberant garden, in that jungle of branches and leaves.

CAROL: It was just a crude set.

SIMON: Naked, so beautiful, untouchable in the center of that jungle.

CAROL: You're talking crazy. Please don't say anymore. It's upsetting me.

SIMON: You can't keep me quiet. I have so many more things to say. This is not just a surface eruption.

CAROL: What are you talking about?

SIMON: This is love coming out at the pores, devouring me, madness, the life force taking me over because of you. Eating me up, gnawing at me.

CAROL: How could you have seen that picture if you were blind?

(*Sound of the train. Silence.*)

SIMON: An intelligent question. Sharp. (*Pause.*) I didn't see it. But they told me about it a thousand times. (*Pause.*) There, in the hospital where I was, your picture made a big splash. The day that someone brought in the magazine with your picture in it, a lot of us... turned a little more sane.

CAROL: In a hospital. Funny.

SIMON: Today is my first day out. After a long time in darkness, I'm coming into the light. And I hope the light will never abandon me again. Not having freedom is something.

CAROL: What... what happened to you? What was wrong with you, if I may ask that?

SIMON: I understood the birds' songs.

CAROL: Is that some kind of mental illness?

SIMON: Seems to be. Yes.

CAROL: Strange, isn't it?

SIMON: Birds say a lot of very interesting things about human beings. Birds listen to everything, they see everything from so high up, with such precision that... (*Pause.*) They know all the little weaknesses of human nature. And who practices them. They know who's wicked, who's mean, who's perverse. They know almost all of them. The dishonest politician, the powerful, the predator. Birds have prodigious memory and keen sensibility. (*Pause.*) First I was indicted for slander. A blind person making accusations about things he can't see or can't have seen is somewhat surprising. And when they ask one for proof, and he says the birds told him, you can imagine! Society, if anything, is very serious. It won't accept birds as witnesses.

CAROL: So that...

SIMON: They decided my mental faculties were disturbed. So they shut me up in a hospital.

(*Silence.*)

CAROL: I think it's wonderful to talk like this, without understanding each other, guessing from our lips what each other is saying. (*Pause.*) You're the kind of man I could let myself fall in love with. I believe in love with every part of my being. Love is the only thing I'm intended for. (*Pause.*) But I beg you, please, don't... don't play with me. I'm... I'm not yet well myself. I've just got through a serious crisis... and I'm recovering... still. This is... funny. A funny coincidence, but this is my first day out too. I'm also coming out of the hospital.

(*Silence.*)

SIMON: Funny coincidence. You're right. Who would have thought? What was wrong with you? Why did they shut you up?

(*Suddenly the noise of tunnels and more tunnels, repeatedly, overwhelms the scene. CAROL's lips can be seen moving, almost imperceptibly, but she can't be heard. Why she was in the hospital will never be known, but some approximate conclusions might be drawn from her gestures which are highly expressive and full of nuance. Then she is still again, quietly observing SIMON. Silence. The sound of the train, clicking along, becomes almost imperceptible.*)

CAROL (*With a serious voice*): I'm falling in love with you. By great leaps and bounds. I'm sorry. I'm sorry I'm telling you this. I don't know if you can hear me with the noise of the train. I don't know if you can understand me either. But in the end it doesn't matter. None of it makes any sense anyway. I need to rest. Definitely. Really rest. My head is aching. You can't imagine the conditions I've been living under the last few years. (*To herself.*) I've got to get hold of myself. Need to remain calm. (*Pause.*) Can you hear me? Do you understand what I'm saying? What are you thinking?

(*Silence. SIMON reaches out and touches CAROL's face with his hand, softly, tracing her features. Then he places his hands on his cane and faces her as if he were observing her.*)

FOSTER (*To HOLMES*): Asleep?
HOLMES: I have my eyes shut, but I'm not asleep.
FOSTER: Have you been listening to our little couple?
HOLMES: No.
FOSTER: Do you understand what they're saying?
HOLMES: No. I don't know what they are, what nationality. Why?
FOSTER: I thought I heard something about a hospital. Mental hospital.
HOLMES: You don't say! A mental hospital. I don't know what that can mean. Why do you find that strange?
FOSTER: It doesn't seem strange to you to hear talk about mental hospitals on a tourist train like this?
HOLMES: It does to you?
FOSTER: It does to me, yes. Because. Well, because I just got out of a hospital myself.

HOLMES: Very interesting. (*Pause.*) What is it that's bothering you?

FOSTER: It just got me thinking about strange things.

HOLMES: That word bothers you so much?

FOSTER: Enough.

HOLMES: You seem nervous. Your hands are shaking. Are you all right? (*Silence.*) You're not going to answer me?

FOSTER: It's like, for a moment, I felt something cold on my face, like a sudden rush of air. Something like a bird fluttering close.

HOLMES: Here? In this compartment?

FOSTER: Here.

HOLMES: Here, as far as I've seen, there's no bird. What are you talking about?

FOSTER: I repeat, I felt something like wings fluttering. And I'm very sensitive about these things. Let's just say from having been ill. The sensitivity of illness. I know something is going on here. I feel it. I sense it. In the air here there's something moving about, something melodic. A certain noise. We're in danger. Something very serious may happen. Death is passing through here, making the rounds. I... I smell it. I can smell it. I feel it. I know it's here.

(*A heavy silence. Something is in fact happening to the ambience, something heavy and palpable.*)

HOLMES: How can you smell death?

FOSTER: Experience. I was a doctor. I've seen hundreds of sick people die. I'm accustomed to it. I've lived close to human suffering for a long time. And I've frequently felt this while sitting at the bedside of someone dying, this same sensation. And I've asked myself before how to explain it. What caused it. This movement of the air. I believe now. You're going to laugh at this. I believe now life is possible because there are angels.

HOLMES: Ah.

FOSTER: Invisible beings who allow life to realize itself, and who can wrap us around with their wings, protecting us, pushing us along. Until one day they take flight, and we're left unprovided for, immobilized, indecisive, condemned to eternal loneliness forever. The kidney drops loose in your abdomen.

HOLMES: What are you talking about?

FOSTER: And it makes a dull sound. And you're dying. It's the end. Today the spleen, tomorrow a lung. Then it's useless to try anymore. It's the end. (*Pause.*) Do you believe in compassion?

HOLMES: I don't know why you ask me that. Yes.

FOSTER: I mean, firmly believe? The way one ought to believe in compassion?

HOLMES: Make your point.

FOSTER: I do. I believe in it. (*Pause.*) Firmly. For me human suffering, when there's no cure, seems monstrous. (*Pause.*) I was a doctor. I had three terminal cases in my ward. All three in unbearable pain. With no possible help. They'd reached the limits of their endurance. But still living. Surviving. (*Pause.*) You can't imagine how long a man will take to die sometimes. And what a terrifying agony the pain of his dying is. (*Pause.*) I killed them. All three of them. I believe that they were profoundly grateful. Intravenous morphine genuinely quiets the pain. And with increased doses it tears it out at the root.

(*Silence.*)

HOLMES: How long did they keep you in there?

FOSTER: Six years. (*Pause.*) And I don't think I could have stood one more day. I have to get to Kiu. To breathe. I'll never be able to live within four walls again. Life without freedom is better not lived. Cut it off. I have great confidence in morphine.

HOLMES: I understand. I was in the place myself for twelve years.

FOSTER: Don't tell me.

HOLMES: Twelve years. Six more than you. Twelve interminable centuries.

FOSTER: What happened to you? Why did they put you there?

HOLMES: For screaming.

FOSTER: For screaming? What do you mean?

HOLMES: I'm not lying. For screaming. A lot. And loud. And mine was not any ordinary, everyday scream. Mine was an explosion, a canon roar. An avalanche of rage rushing from my throat. My son was beaten to death by police with nightsticks. (*Pause.*) Don't you think that's a good reason to scream?

FOSTER: Of course.

HOLMES: It was his first year at the university. The autopsy showed that a blood clot had formed in his brain as a consequence of a blow to the head. It took him half an hour to die. It was just a little political demonstration by some students. Something innocent. But it cost him his life. (*Pause.*) I went to the Chief of Police. I took a letter of protest signed by a lot of parents, against violence. (*Pause.*) I remember they made me wait a while. I went into some office. When I saw him there in front of me, when I was about to hand him the letter. I don't know what happened. It was like I had a mouthful of acid. Without knowing why, I started to scream, right in his face, at his eyes, at his mouth. And I followed him out into the street, and I screamed. And I screamed there outside the Presidential Palace! I screamed, one day, two, three days. And a whole chorus formed. (*Smiles.*) They detained me. When they let me go, I went right back, to the same door, one hour, two. Weeks, months. You know, when a man is really determined to scream about something, it's very hard to shut him up. The power of a scream is immeasurable. It doesn't require spilling a single drop of blood. And immediately other voices join in, lines of people form, choruses, crowds of the just, and only violence can silence them.

(*The noise of the train. Tunnels. Freezing wind.*)

FOSTER: How did they diagnose you?
HOLMES: They kept changing the diagnosis. Schizophrenia. Neurosis. Paranoia. Finally they opted for calling it vociferating depression. They couldn't come up with anything better. (*Pause.*) I don't think I could have stood one more day either. I feel exhausted. (*Pause.*) I don't have any concrete idea of Kiu either. I'm not sure if it's on the coast or in the mountains. But in the end it's all the same. In the hospital they told me it was a little paradise. They were even kind enough to get me the ticket and accompany me to the station.
FOSTER: The same with me. (*Pause.*) They also talked to me a lot about Kiu. (*Pause.*) You know something? I'd like to be your friend.

(*After a few moments of silence HOLMES takes out a cigarette and hands it to FOSTER, then lights it for him. They smoke in silence. A certain closeness has developed between the two men. By this time day is slowly dawning. Light increases in the compartment to full sun. The sound of birds. There has been a radical change in the climate. It begins to get hot. The air is clear. From the reflections of light on the faces and across the seats one gets the sense that outside, with the start of day, an exuberant nature is awakening. CAROL and SIMON, who have remained practically motionless in the semi-darkness, now turn toward FOSTER and HOLMES. Someone stretches.*)

FOSTER: Do you two know where we are?
CAROL: No.
SIMON: Is it daylight?
CAROL: Yes.

FOSTER: How much longer will it be? (*Pause. He stretches his legs.*) Aren't you hot?

CAROL: A little.

FOSTER: If you don't mind, I'm going to open the window. The air is a little stuffy. (*He gets up and tries to open the window without success.*) Come on! It's locked.

(*There is a strange silence. They look at each other. SIMON stretches his neck forward listening intently. HOLMES, serious, gets up and, with a certain violence, tries opening the window, also without success. He hits the glass. Silence. They all look at each other.*)

CAROL: And that one?

SIMON: The window won't open?

CAROL: It seems to be locked.

(*HOLMES goes to the door of the compartment and pulls hard on it but without opening it.*)

HOLMES: Now... what's this all about?

SIMON: It won't open?

HOLMES: Seems that way. (*Looking at the latch.*) We're locked in here! This door is locked with a key. On the outside!

(*Silence.*)

FOSTER: My God! No!

CAROL: What? Locked?

(*HOLMES starts beating and kicking the door. He lets out a shout, and BABINSKI appears in the corridor.*)

BABINSKI (*From the corridor*): Quiet! Quiet in there!

HOLMES: Open this door immediately!

BABINSKI (*Smiling through the window*): What? You want me to open it? (*Refusing sarcastically with his head.*) Impossible. This door doesn't open. It's a door. But it's missing its reason for being. So now it's a wall. A transparent wall, with a window, but unbreakable. (*Pause.*) Sorry.

HOLMES (*Hitting the glass*): Listen!

BABINSKI: The door will remain locked! Silence! I have no intention of allowing the least disruption of order on this train! I'm authorized to keep order!

FOSTER: No!

CAROL: What is he talking about? Keep order?

FOSTER (*Livid but without strength, understanding the situation*): I demand... I demand an explanation. You can't do this.

BABINKSI: Oh can't I? Where did you think you were going, you stupid fools? On a pleasure trip? Some resort, right? What did they tell you, you miserable lot? Fools? (*Pause.*) You're going to the maximum security hospital at Kiu! Idiots!

FOSTER: No. (*He slumps in his seat. SIMON passes his hand across his brow. CAROL closes her eyes.*)

BABINSKI: A big concrete hole surrounded by swamps! No birds, no beaches, no mountains, no exit! That's where you're headed! Fools! What did you want them to tell you about Kiu? That it's an infected cesspool?

HOLMES: Oh.

BABINSKI: Oh my, what faces! So finally it sunk in, huh? What? It doesn't suit you? It's not possible. You all look a little trainsick. What sad pusses. (*To SIMON.*) And you look like you've heard this too, right?. Or maybe not. Want me to say it again louder? O.K.? Want to know what there really is in Kiu? Well... a prison madhouse, my dear, for the highly dangerous sick. You understand? A cube of concrete, no windows, no air, high, indestructible, impregnable walls, stained by the hatred of those inside rotting away. (*Mopping sweat, chewing his cigar. Silence. SIMON has gone back to his earlier position, opposite CAROL, sitting up straight, apparently unperturbed, his hands on the top of his cane.*) You hear me, insect? You hear me now? Say something! Answer me, pig! Or doesn't it matter to you? If I come in there it'll matter. If I come in there, I'll roast you, you son of a...

(*He rushes off down the corridor, raging, fists clenched, mopping sweat, and leaving a stinking cloud of cigar smoke. A heavy silence. The heat increases. Noise of birds. From time to time SIMON turns his head slightly as if paying attention to something. FOSTER huddles up in a corner and covers his head with his jacket. His eyes have been tight shut since BABINSKI's telling them where they're going. HOLMES's gaze seems lost on some distant point, his jaws are clenched in severe pain and anger.*)

HOLMES (*In a sort of unintelligible litany*): Traitors. Swine. Degenerates. (*Pause.*) Traitors. Swine. Scum. Murderers. Sons of bitches.

(*CAROL puts her sunglasses on again.*)

SIMON: Are you crying?
CAROL: No.
SIMON: What have you done? Why did you move?
CAROL: I've put my sunglasses on. (*Pause.*) My glasses are so dark... so completely dark... that I can't even make out shapes. It's rather pleasant.

(*Silence.*)

SIMON: Your're sad?
CAROL: A little. I needed so much to rest. I'd thought so much about this trip. They'd talked to me so much about Kiu.
SIMON: Don't cry, please.
CAROL: I'm not crying.
SIMON: Yes, you are crying. (*CAROL silently sneaks a finger under her glasses and wipes away a tear. Silence.*) Don't cry. Please, I beg you.

(*He reaches out and tenderly wipes away a tear. CAROL takes SIMON's hand. He gives a start as if shocked. She caresses his hand softly. Her expression is one of deep sadness. She continues crying silently.*)

SIMON: Please.
CAROL: I'm sorry.

(*She lets go of his hand. They remain facing each other, both with their dark glasses, so dark that no light seems to get through. The train brakes slightly. FOSTER, all at once, tips forward, sways for a moment in an unsteady equilibrium, then falls heavily to the floor. His entire shirt is covered with blood, and deep cuts show on his arms. A scream from CAROL. HOLMES bends down trying to lift him. He is dead. BABINSKI appears in the corridor, brought on by CAROL's scream.*)

BABINSKI (*Yelling*): Doctor! Doctor!

(*He opens the door. HOLMES, on seeing the door open, throws himself on BABINSKI, striking him hard across the face, trying to get out. The*

DOCTOR and a brute of an ASSISTANT appear. They subdue HOLMES and put him down, the ASSISTANT giving him a rabbit punch on the back of the neck. He falls down unconscious. They put a straight jacket on him. The DOCTOR listens to FOSTER's heart and examines his pupils.)

DOCTOR (*To ASSISTANT*): He's dead. Get him out of here. He's slashed both arms.

(*The ASSISTANT drags FOSTER out.*)

SIMON: Please.

DOCTOR: Silence! Absolute silence! Everyone calm down. Nothing has happened. We'll be in Kiu very shortly. (*Mopping his brow, extremely nervous.*) Everything was going so well. (*To BABINSKI.*) How are you? Did he hurt you?

BABINSKI (*Stopping his bleeding without taking his eyes off the unconscious HOLMES*): It's nothing. I'm used to this stuff.

DOCTOR: Let me take a look at you.

BABINSKI (*Red with anger*): You know what I say to you, Doctor?

DOCTOR: What's the matter with you?

BABINSKI: Go take a look at your old man. Keep your hands off me!

DOCTOR: You're all upset.

BABINSKI (*Pointing at HOLMES*): The next time one of these crazy nuts puts his hands on me. I swear I'll run him straight through. You hear me? And to hell with whatever you think you're going to report to your superiors, Doctor! Because I've had it! My last trip! You hear me? I've had a bellyfull of you people. They can shove their high risk bonus up their ass!

DOCTOR: This is not the time.

BABINSKI: The hell it isn't! (*Gives the still unconscious HOLMES a kick.*) I swear, I'll kill him. If he lifts a hand... (*He leaves slamming the compartment door.*)

ASSISTANT (*Indicating FOSTER*): What do I do with this one?

DOCTOR: With this one? You're asking me! Throw him out the window if you like! Now I'm the one who's upset! Put him in the funeral car! And if this filthy train doesn't have a funeral car like all the other trains in the world, then turn something into one! Open a compartment and light a couple candles. And nighty night! Please! You're giving me a heart attack! Don't bother me!

(He leaves. The ASSISTANT drags the body out and down the corridor. The door remains locked. Noise of the train. Insufferable heat. Suddenly, at just the right moment, the sounds of birds, previously interspersed as a counterpoint to the noise of the train, become much louder, more strident, and harsh. Several birds, as if terrified, crash against the outside windows. SIMON reacts as if he were being jolted by electrical charges. He stands and stretches his neck in every direction listening intently. He slowly sits down again, perspiring.)

CAROL: Something's happening to you. Are you all right? *(Silence.)* What are you thinking about?
SIMON: About you.
CAROL: You're perspiring.

(She dries his brow. He reacts with surprise and appears agitated.)

SIMON: Will you promise me something?
CAROL: I don't understand. What do you mean?
SIMON: I know how to get you out of this.
CAROL: How?
SIMON: But you have to do everything I say.
CAROL: What?
SIMON: There's no time to lose. Listen carefully. You have to...
CAROL: But...
SIMON: No! Listen, there's no time to lose. In a minute the train will stop. It's the last station before Kiu. When I tell you, you have to run to the door, open it, and jump. As fast as you can. Without looking back. You hear?
CAROL: Yes.
SIMON: When I say: Now! You have to get out of here running! You hear? Open the door and jump. Down to the platform! As fast as you can! *(The train whistles and starts to brake. CAROL looks at SIMON. He is tense and charged.)* You hear me?
CAROL: I hear you.
SIMON: I... I... *(He swallows.)*

(The train is slowing coming to a stop. SIMON beats on the door with his cane.)

SIMON: Help! Please, help!
BABINSKI *(Coming down the corridor in a foul humor)*: What's going on?

SIMON: I would like to relieve myself, please. I can't wait any longer. Will you go with me? Will you take my arm, please.?

(*BABINSKI takes him by the arm. The train comes to a stop.*)

SIMON: Believe me, I'm sorry about earlier. I didn't do that on purpose. (*To CAROL*) Now!

(*CAROL breaks away running down the corridor. SIMON pulls out the stiletto-handle of his cane and drives the blade into BABINSKI's chest. BABINSKI crumples to the floor as if struck by lightning, a cry starting from his throat. A door-slam is heard. The DOCTOR and ASSISTANT appear. SIMON inserts the blade back into his cane and sits down again, hands on cane, impassive.*)

SIMON: I'm sorry.

(*BLACKOUT.*)

(*When the lights come up, SIMON and HOLMES are seated facing each other, both with straight jackets on. The DOCTOR and ASSISTANT, cautious and obviously worried, are both in the compartment.*)

DOCTOR: The authorities will get a full accounting of this. I don't intend to leave out a single detail. Legal shenanigans are not going to protect you two. You're not crazy. Not at all! You're born insubordinates. You're brutes. Violent psychopaths. Murderers. That's what you are! (*Close to losing control, he wipes away sweat.*) A great trip you've given me. Two dead and one on the loose. Brawling. Scandalous! Blood and psychopharmaceuticals. Yes, and for sure, one thing. You must both be horses. The amount of barbiturate I shot into you, you ought to be in a coma.

SIMON: Doctor.

DOCTOR: Forget doctor! Shut up! Nothing! Not a word. I don't want to hear a word! Murder! One false move, one hint of violence, I swear to God, I'll use the chloroform. (*He takes a bottle from his pocket.*) This is going to cost you. Plenty. (*He fans himself with a newspaper.*) God, look at me, I'm soaked. Damned sweat! You've got me over the edge. And I have not been over the edge for years. (*Holding his hand out.*) Look how I'm shaking. You happy now! What you've done. Your conduct is disgraceful, gentlemen. You've conducted yourselves like genuine sons of bitches.

SIMON: Doctor.

DOCTOR: Nothing! Nothing! Nothing! I said: nothing! (*Stamping on the floor.*) I've got to calm down. I can't arrive at the station like this. I've got to explain this whole thing, in detail. Even then they won't believe me. Got to figure out how to put it. If my voice is shaking, they'll think it's the same as if I... if I...

ASSISTANT: Doctor.

DOCTOR: Shut up! (*Realizing who spoke.*) Sorry. I'm very nervous. You, yes. What is it?

ASSISTANT: I think.

DOCTOR: Come on, out with it! What are you waiting for?

(*The ASSISTANT whispers something in his ear. The DOCTOR breaks out laughing.*)

DOCTOR: You would like to take a piss! Right now? Right this very minute, which is exactly when I need you most. Well, hold it! Or don't you know that at any moment these two could jump us and tear out our eyes? I also am about to piss myself. For the whole last hour. And I have not said a word. Look.

ASSISTANT: What?

DOCTOR: Drops of urine! My bladder is about to burst!

(*Suddenly the noise of the birds becomes sharply louder, more strident, thudding, terrified, against the windows like lumps of meat.*)

DOCTOR (*Shouting*): What is that?

ASSISTANT: I don't know what's happening. (*Looking out the window.*) They're going crazy.

DOCTOR: And I just pissed all over myself! Just what I needed! Look at me, I'm soaked! What are they going to think of me when I get there?

ASSISTANT: And me? (*Feeling down between his legs.*)

DOCTOR: You too?

ASSISTANT: It was the scare.

(*Another wave of strident sounds, and more birds bang against the window. The DOCTOR lets out another scream. Silence. A pitiful look on the DOCTOR's face.*)

SIMON: Something smells like a stinking plague.

DOCTOR: Silence!
SIMON: No one can stand that smell. The window!
DOCTOR: I said silence!

(*The ASSISTANT covers his nose and looks at the DOCTOR.*)

ASSISTANT: Doctor.
DOCTOR (*Embarrassed*): You too?
ASSISTANT: Are we almost to Kiu?
DOCTOR: I don't know. This is my first trip to Kiu! And my last! Because as soon as we get there, I'm catching the next train out, and I'm going back to my mother's where I ought to be right now! In my own town, in my own room, in my own bed, resting! God damn the day I ever took this job! Better to be without one. I don't know the first thing about psychiatry! I'm a dermatologist! I've never given an injection in my life!
SIMON: I can tell.
DOCTOR: You have something to say?
SIMON: You know what the birds are calling you?
DOCTOR: Me? The birds?
SIMON: A lump of shit.
DOCTOR: Really? How charming! A lump of shit. And how do you happen to know this?
SIMON: Because I understand the language of the birds.
DOCTOR: Ha, ha, ha! You understand the language of the birds. And I talk to turtles! (*A slightly hysterical laugh.*) I'll never get out of here a normal person. My nerves are shot. It's a contagious mania.
ASSISTANT: I'm getting sick. I'm sorry. The smell.

(*Retching, he rushes from the compartment, quickly lowers a window in the corridor, leans out, and starts vomiting. HOLMES, who has remained all this time with his eyes closed, as if unconscious, suddenly leaps up, runs from the compartment, and throws himself through the open window. There is a thin scream. The DOCTOR crosses and looks out the window, then comes back and falls heavily on to the seat, his head in his hands. The ASSISTANT, looking pale, comes back in and sits down. The DOCTOR attacks him furiously, slapping him about and screaming.*)

DOCTOR: I was just telling you! Don't get sick! Don't open the window! These people are dangerous! Do it all over yourself. Vomit all over yourself. That's what I was telling you! (*Pause.*) Poor man. He was busted to pieces. The telephone pole decapitated him. (*Pause. He covers his face.*) Another one. And another one! And another one! (*Hitting himself on the head.*) The only thing left is for something to happen to us. And I'll never see my mother again. (*Begins crying.*)

SIMON: Do you believe in love, Doctor?

DOCTOR (*Breaking into hysterical laughter*): You kill me! You kill me laughing! Believe in love? Under these circumstances . When a man just left his brains all over a telephone pole. When we've just spread the road with dead bodies! Believe in love? And why not believe in the gall bladder? Or, ah... or in God? Right! Why not bring God into this, I mean, heh?

SIMON: And in hope, Doctor? Do you firmly believe, the way one has to believe, in hope?

(*A terrible noise of birds, furious and wild.*)

DOCTOR: These damned birds! These damned, disgusting pests!

SIMON: I do. I firmly believe.

DOCTOR: Shut up, you... deformity! Garbage! You're the worst of the lot. You're a criminal. You stabbed a defenseless man to death! You!

(*Noise of the birds. The DOCTOR covers his ears. The ASSISTANT looks around in amazement. The DOCTOR gets up, on the verge of collapse, and lets out a scream. Silence.*)

DOCTOR (*Astonished, looking out the window*): They've gone quiet. They've all gone quiet. Why would they go quiet? Why the silence?

(*Thick, heavy, overwhelming silence.*)

SIMON: No use now.

DOCTOR: What do you mean?

SIMON: You'll never see your mother again, Doctor.

DOCTOR: Why?

SIMON: You're going to die.

DOCTOR (*Frightened*): Explain yourself.

SIMON: I tell you. It's already too late. The train is going to jump the rails. That's what they've been saying all this time.

(*Silence.*)

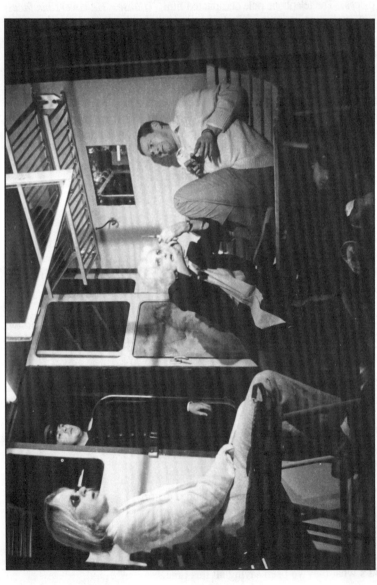

Pnervocryste zero (El cero transparente). Teatr Dramatyezny, Plock, Poland, 1990. Photo: Waldemar Lawendowski.

SIMON: Birds are surprising creatures. You see, they don't wear clothes, but no creatures are better clothed. They have dominion over the air. And dominion over the earth with their winging, ethereal flight. Constantly protecting the weak, helping them in the sordid struggle against the strong, and the dark. (*Standing.*) My love. My love. My angel. I'll follow you, loving you, constantly, eternally.

(*Suddenly CAROL appears coming slowly along the corridor. She has not jumped from the train but has remained hidden aboard. She turns toward the compartment as if hypnotized and charged by the presence of this mysterious blind man who understands the language of the birds. SIMON is unaware of her presence but continues to speak in her direction.*)

SIMON: I don't know if you can hear me over the noise of the train. Or if you can understand me by the movement of my lips. So far from me now as you must be. So far from me now when I need you. Now as I start towards death.

(*Silence.*)

CAROL: Simon...

(*SIMON turns his head towards where her voice sounded. The noise of a train jumping the rails amidst sparks, screams, and voices. Then silence. CAROL and SIMON are seen in an almost complete semi-darkness, standing motionless.*)

CRITICAL REACTION TO VALLEJO'S WORK

"The work produces in us the same anguish that a great poem does. We painfully cross through cruelty, loneliness, formulisms, death; but far from surrendering to the 'naturalness' of the cycle, we free, from the depths of our being, some other crouching personality whose inexorable brilliance stands up against that 'natural order of the world.'"

José Monleón
El cero transparente (Preface)
Editorial Fundamentos
Madrid, 1978

"Vallejo is an author of a pure theater...derived from the theater of the absurd with a power and personality which no one except Arrabal has shown."

Antonio Valencia
Hoja de Lunes

"The author of our time best qualified to break through the hard shell of realism and create a clear, clean, and effective system of communication. Nothing less."

Enrique Llovet
Cangrejos de pared (Prologue)

"[*Train to Kiu*] is a different kind of theater, a coherently structured text in which surprise is the determining factor."
"For me Alfonso Vallejo...demonstrates that the Spanish theater has found an original playwright, violent, cruel, lyric, an ultrasensitive realist, mysterious and diaphanous, intelligent, and with his own cosmos into which he wishes to tie us through an investigative pleasure..."

Carlos García-Osuna
El Imparcial

ABOUT THE TRANSLATOR

H. Rick Hite is Professor of Theater/Communications at Virginia Wesleyan College. While his professional work and teaching is principally in theater (directing and acting) and theater literature, he holds degrees in Spanish from Dartmouth College and The Johns Hopkins University and was Fulbright Lecturer in Spain in 1974/75. Among his translations which have had performances are Alejandro Casona's *Siren Cast Ashore (La sirena varada)*, Alfonso Vallejo's *Weekend*, and Fermín Cabal's *Get Thee Behind Me! (¡Vade retro!)* and *Passage (Travesía)*

TRANSLATOR'S ACKNOWLEDGMENTS

I acknowledge a long-standing debt of gratitude to Martha Halsey, infinitely patient and efficacious editor of this series, and to Phyllis Zatlin for her invaluable advice in the preparation of this translation. My thanks go also to Judy Kelly, Professor of Drama at the University of Dallas, for her cooperation and interest in the performance of plays by Spanish authors. I also thank Robert Dixon for his conscientious attention in preparing the camera-ready copy for this volume.

ESTRENO: CONTEMPORARY SPANISH PLAYS SERIES

General Editor: Martha T. Halsey

No. 1 Jaime Salom: *Bonfire at Dawn* (*Una hoguera al amanecer*)
Translated by Phyllis Zatlin. 1992.   ISBN: 0-9631212-0-0

No. 2 José López Rubio: *In August We Play the Pyrenees* (*Celos del aire*)
Translated by Marion P. Holt. 1992.   ISBN: 0-9631212-1-9

No. 3 Ramón del Valle-Inclán: *Savage Acts: Four Plays* (*Ligazón, La rosa de papel, La cabeza del Bautista, Sacrilegio*) Translated by Robert Lima. 1993.   ISBN: 0-9631212-2-7

No. 4 Antonio Gala: *The Bells of Orleans* (*Los buenos días perdidos*)
Translated by Edward Borsoi. 1993.   ISBN: 0-9631212-3-5

No. 5 Antonio Buero-Vallejo: *The Music Window* (*Música cercana*)
Translated by Marion P. Holt. 1994.   ISBN: 0-9631212-4-3

No. 6 Paloma Pedrero: *Parting Gestures: Three by Pedrero* (*El color de agosto, La noche dividida, Resguardo personal*) Translated by Phyllis Zatlin. 1994.   ISBN: 0-9631212-5-1

No. 7 Ana Diosdado: *Yours for the Asking* (*Usted también podrá disfrutar de ella*)
Translated by Patricia W. O'Connor. 1995.   ISBN: 0-9631212-6-X

No. 9 Alfonso Vallejo: *Train to Kiu* (*El cero transparente*)
Translated by H. Rick Hite. 1996.   ISBN: 0-9631212-8-6

A continuing series representing Spanish plays of several generations and varying theatrical approaches,
selected for their potential interest to American audiences. Published every 6-9 months.

- -

SUBSCRIPTION/ORDER FORM

Check one:

_____ Standing order for play series. (May be cancelled at any time if desired.)
       $6.00 including postage, to be billed when you receive your copy.

_____ Individual play/s. Prepaid. $6.00 including postage. List titles and quantities below:

_____   _____

_____   _____

_____   _____

Name and address: _____

                     _____

                     _____

Mail to: ESTRENO   Telephone: 814/865-1122
          350 N. Burrowes Bldg.   FAX: 814/863-7944
          University Park, PA 16802 USA

ESTRENO: OFERTA ESPECIAL

1	Ejemplar ....$13.00 ejemplar	Más de 10 ejemplares ....$ 7.00 ejemplar	
2-5	Ejemplares ....$10.00 ejemplar	Colección completa..........$ 6.00 ejemplar	
6-10	Ejemplares ....$8.00 ejemplar		

Vol. 1, *	No. 1 (1975)	Jerónimo López Mozo: **Guernica.**
Vol. 1, *	No. 2 (1975)	Romeo de Esteo: **Paraphernalia de la olla podrida, la misericordia y la mucha compasión.**
Vol. 1, *	No. 3 (1975)	Martínez Ballesteros: **Los placeres de la egregia dama.**
Vol. 2,	No. 1 (1976)	Arrabal: **El arquitecto y el emperador de Asiria.**
Vol. 2,	No. 2 (1976)	Lauro Olmo: **José García.**
Vol. 3,	No. 1 (1977)	Martín Recuerda: **La llanura.**
Vol. 3,	No. 2 (1977)	Ricardo Morales: **La imagen.**
Vol. 4,	No. 1 (1978)	Buero Vallejo: **La detonación.**
Vol. 4,	No. 2 (1978)	José López Rubio: **El último hilo.**
Vol. 5,	No. 1 (1979)	"**Buero Vallejo a través de los años**"
Vol. 5,	No. 2 (1979)	Jordi Teixidor: **La jungla sentimental.**
Vol. 6,	No. 1 (1980)	**Encuesta sobre el teatro madrileño de los años 70.**
Vol. 6,	No. 2 (1980)	Manuel Martínez Mediero: **Las hermanas de Búfalo Bill.**
Vol. 7,	No. 1 (1981)	García Alvarez y Pedro Muñoz Seca: **La casa de los crímenes.**
Vol. 7,	No. 2 (1981)	Pedro Salinas: **Los santos.**
Vol. 8, *	No. 1 (1982)	Luis Riaza: **Antígona...Cerda.**
Vol. 8,	No. 2 (1982)	Jaime Salom: **La gran aventura.**
Vol. 9,	No. 1 (1983)	Alfonso Sastre: **El hijo único de Guillermo Tell.**
Vol. 9,	No. 2 (1983)	Jorge Díaz: **Educación y un ombligo para dos.**
Vol. 10,	No. 1 (1984)	Víctor Ruiz Iriarte: **Juanita va a a Río de Janeiro.**

Vol. 10,	No. 2	(1984)	Lidia Falcón: **No moleste, calle y pague.**
Vol. 11,	No. 1	(1985)	Carmen Resino: **Ultimar detalles.**
Vol. 11,	No. 2	(1985)	Antonio Gala: **El veredicto.**
Vol. 12,	No. 1	(1986)	José Luis Alonso de Santos: **Del laberinto al 30.**
Vol. 12,	No. 2	(1986)	María Aurelia Capmany: **Tú y el hipócrita.**
Vol. 13,	No. 1	(1987)	Antonio Martínez Ballesteros: **Los comediantes.**
Vol. 13,	No. 2	(1987)	**Encuesta sobre el teatro de Valle-Inclán**
Vol. 14,	No. 1	(1988)	**Artículos sobre Buero,teatro postfranquista.**
Vol. 14,	No. 2	(1988)	Domingo Miras: **El doctor Torralba.** **"Modern Spanish Drama on the Professional English-Speaking Stage"** (Número monográfico).
Vol. 15,	No. 1	(1989)	**Entrevista con Sastre, artículos sobre Carmen Resino, Lourdes Ortiz, Salom y Valle-Inclán** Francisco Nieva: **Te quiero, zorra.**
Vol. 15,	No. 2	(1989)	**La mujer: autora y personaje.** (Número monográfico)
Vol. 16,	No. 1	(1990)	**Teatro español en Inglaterra, EEUU y Francia.**
Vol. 16,	No. 2	(1990)	Antonio Onetti: **La puñalá.**
Vol. 17,	No. 1	(1991)	Carlos Muñiz: **El caballo del caballero.**
Vol. 17,	No. 2	(1991)	**Teatro español e hispanoamericano.**
Vol. 18,	No. 1	(1992)	Antonio Gala: **Cristóbal Colón.**
Vol. 18,	No. 2	(1992)	Eduardo Quiles: **Una Ofelia sin Hamlet.**
Vol. 19,	No. 1	(1993)	Eduardo Galán Font: **La posada del arenal.**
Vol. 19,	No. 2	(1993)	José M. Rodríguez Méndez: **Isabelita tiene ángel.**
Vol. 20,	No. 1	(1993)	Concha Romero: **Allá él**
Vol. 20,	No. 2	(1994)	Jorge Díaz: **Historia de nadie**
Vol. 21,	No. 1	(1995)	Buero Vallejo: **Las trampas del azar**
Vol. 21,	No. 2	(1995)	Lauro Olmo: **El perchero**
Vol. 22,	No. 1	(1996)	Jaime Salom: **Una noche con Clark Gable**
Vol. 22,	No. 2	(1996)	

* **Agotados. Hay fotocopias disponibles a la venta**

City _____ State _____ Zip _____

Address _____

Name _____

___ Institutions US$30/year   ___ Individuals US$15/year

Please Mail to: Center of Latin American Studies
107 Lippincott Hall, KU • Lawrence, Kansas 66045

LATIN AMERICAN THEATRE REVIEW

ISSN 0023-8813

since 1967

Analyses of Dramatic Works
Interviews with Playwrights
Performance Reviews
Theatre Festival Updates
Current Annotated Bibliography
Book Reviews of New Works on Drama

Center of Latin American Studies
University of Kansas

A Journal devoted

to the Theatre and Drama of

Spanish and Portuguese America

ESTRENO:
CUADERNOS DEL TEATRO
ESPAÑOL CONTEMPORANEO

Published at Penn State University
Martha Halsey, Ed.
Phyllis Zatlin, Assoc. Ed.

A journal featuring play texts of previously unpublished works from contemporary Spain, interviews withplaywrights, directors, and critics, and extensive critical studies in both Spanish and English.

Plays published have included texts by Buero-Vallejo, Sastre, Arrabal, Gala, Nieva, Salom, Martín Recuerda, Olmo, Martínez Mediero, F. Cabal, P. Pedrero and Onetti. The journal carries numerous photographs of recent play performances in Spain and elsewhere, including performances in translation.

Also featured are an annual bibliography, regular book reviews, and critiques of the recent theater season, as well as a round table in which readers from both the U. S. and Spain share information and engage in lively debates.

ESTRENO also publishes a series of translations of contemporary Spanish plays which may be subscribed to separately.

Please mail to: ESTRENO
350 N. Burrowes Bldg.
University Park, PA 16802
USA.

Individual subscriptions are $15.00 and institutional subscriptions, $26.00 for the calendar year.

Name _____

Address _____

_____